5 Steps to the Statement of Purpose

A short guide to writing a personal statement for admission to a US graduate program in the humanities

by

Arthur William Wright

Contents

Why *five* steps?

The statement of purpose for graduate school in the humanities is an odd genre. The SOP, as it's often called, is the sort of text you're likely to write once—maybe twice. After that, you'll be writing other sorts of documents: seminar papers, a doctoral dissertation, academic articles, perhaps even an academic book or two. The statement of purpose, then, is the kind of document you'll agonize over, revise, submit, and then forget.

Because most people have limited experience writing a statement of purpose, potential applicants often lack qualified mentors to help them write their own statements. Even accomplished professors have only written their own statements once or twice, and not all professors serve on graduate program admissions committees. This problem is compounded for students applying from outside the United States. The conventions of the US academy are very different from those of Europe, Asia, or Africa. Not knowing exactly what the statement of purpose audience is looking for, applicants often leave important questions unanswered. The admissions committee, then, is left confused about an applicant's scholarly trajectory, her particular focus, her past accomplishments, her ultimate aims, and her fit with the program to which she's applying.

These five answers—trajectory, focus, accomplishments, aims, and fit—are the key to writing a statement of purpose for a US graduate program in the humanities. I make clear that these are particular to the United States, in part, because UK and European postgraduate programs—and many of the Asian and African graduate programs that are modelled on them—rely on very different criteria for admissions. In the United Kingdom, for instance, applicants to a Ph.D. apply to work with a particular academic advisor on a particular dissertation project. As a result, applications must indicate how the applicant's aims will align with one particular scholar for one particular project, the dissertation. But in the United States, applicants do not apply to work exclusively with a single scholar, nor do they apply with a fully articulated dissertation project in mind. Instead, they apply to an entire department to work on an interrelated set of questions. A dissertation project will emerge from the study of these questions.

A humanities Ph.D. program in the United States typically takes five or six years to complete. For the first two years, a student will take classes. In the third year, the student will read widely and prepare for a comprehensive examination. This process culminates in the submission of dissertation prospectus, or plan. Then, during the student's remaining time in the program, she or he will write the dissertation. The course of study culminates in the dissertation "defense," a formal review by the student's three- or four-member committee, as well as one or more outside readers.

The graduate admissions committee, then, is looking for candidates who will succeed at each step of the process: completing coursework, preparing for the comprehensive examination, and writing the dissertation. They are also looking for junior scholars who will become excellent colleagues in five or six years. Does the applicant have a vision for the kind of scholarship she will write in the future? Does she have a clear sense of what kind of scholar she hopes to become? And, perhaps most importantly, does the scholarship she has written in the past, as a student, demonstrate that she will be able to grow into an interesting, capable member of the academic profession?

There are five ways to demonstrate that you meet these criteria, and the following guide will take you step-by-step through this process.

In my work advising graduate students—who have gone on to humanities graduate programs at several elite universities—I have found that attention to these five criteria enable applicants to succeed. Indeed, many have written five-paragraph statements of purpose, devoting one paragraph to each question. That is not a requirement, of course, but it is often a helpful way to begin.

Ideally, you'll begin writing your graduate school statement of purpose over the summer prior to the application season.

Graduate program applications in the United States are typically due between December and February, although some deadlines are slightly earlier or later. Most decisions by graduate programs come through in February or March. Then, applicants typically have until April 15 to make a final determination about which program they will attend.

As an applicant, you'll need to complete many tasks: revising your writing sample, soliciting recommendations from at least three former professors, writing any additional materials, such as a diversity statement, and completing standardized tests (such as the GRE or TOEFL). This will take an enormous amount of time. But the statement of purpose is the key to your application. It is your chance to make clear to the admissions committee why they should admit you to their program. It must be clearly written, compelling, and comprehensive. You will have to revise your statement many times.

The following guide, then, is meant to help you to begin this process. After reading this guide, you should be prepared to write an excellent first draft. After that, you should solicit the advice of mentors, colleagues, and friends. And you should ask them whether you are adequately answering the five questions outlined here. The admissions committee will be looking for the answers to these questions, and you should do your best to provide them.

Step One
Trajectory

In my experience, "trajectory" is for most applicants the most difficult element of the statement of purpose to articulate. Your scholarly "trajectory" is the path by which you move from your past scholarly focus to your future scholarly focus. It is the process by which the scholar you have been will transition into the scholar you will be. It's easiest to picture this "trajectory" with concrete examples.

Let's say, for instance, that you want to study the counter-Enlightenment when you are in graduate school. This movement of reactionary intellectuals in the late eighteenth and early nineteenth centuries has been studied in the departments of history, philosophy, political science, and literature, among others. But you plan to enroll in a history Ph.D. program. The trouble is that you were a philosophy major as an undergraduate. You may have many reasons for transitioning from philosophy to history. Maybe you didn't like the culture of the philosophy department. Maybe you had a particularly good relationship with a history professor, or a particularly bad one with several philosophy professors or students. But, in your statement of purpose, you will do your best to articulate the *intellectual* reasons for this transition, rather than your personal reasons. In essence, you will explain how a philosophy background led you to your interest in the history of the counter-Enlightenment.

You might focus on how the Enlightenment and the counter-Enlightenment are taught in philosophy unmoored from their historical circumstances. The work of Hagel is taught in relation to Rousseau, not in relation to what Hagel read in the newspaper or what he ate for breakfast. But you think that historical particularity—the material conditions of a philosopher's life, for instance—exerts a shaping influence on his or her philosophy. Your background in philosophy, then, is an advantage as you move into a new area of scholarly inquiry, history. But you also have a great deal to learn about historicist methods. In short,

6

you have a strong background in one field and room for growth in another.

Consider, alternatively, that you're interested in studying the emergence of "viral" forms of media, and you want to pursue this study in a literature Ph.D. program. You were a literature student as an undergraduate—you majored in English—but the courses you took didn't really prepare you to study the history of viral media. You have a vague sense that newspaper stories in the nineteenth century went "viral," and you think that it's important to understand this viral media today. You've identified a few scholars in literature programs who do this work, and you'd like to enroll in one of their programs. Your concern, though, is that you mostly just read poetry as an undergraduate. Your task, then, is to turn this seeming weakness into a strength. You're interested in viral media, how lines of verse or stories compel people, and how they get repurposed and reused. Your past interest in verse, then, has prepared you for your future interest in viral media. You have spent time thinking about how language is constructed. You have spent time thinking about how poets borrow from earlier poets. You have spent time thinking about what makes a short snippet of language compelling, or interesting, or even catchy. As you articulate your trajectory, then, you will focus on how this past study of verse will enable you to think differently about the kind of language that gets transmitted over networks of information.

These are only two potential examples. My point is that your first task is to identify for your reader where you're coming from and where you're going. Then, you'll make clear the path between these two points. Often, applicants think about their past training as a site of weakness. They worry that they haven't taken the right courses, or that they haven't worked with the right professors. In the humanities, however, there is no "right" preparation. The task of a humanist is to think differently about the conditions of the human. What might it mean, the humanist asks, to consider computer programming from the standpoint of moral philosophy? Or to consider the emergence of ballet in seventeenth-century France from the perspective of the French empire? Whatever experience you do bring to your studies can be a strength. Your task, then, is to articulate how your unique background will be a strength as you embark upon your next course of research.

In the United States, many students have written a "personal statement" for admission to an undergraduate program. The subject of this statement is the student's character and personality. In the undergraduate personal statement, students often tell a story about where they came from. The graduate school statement of purpose is very different. As a potential graduate student, you will not be disclosing details about your personal life: your friendships, your family relationships, or your romantic life.

That said, it often *is* appropriate to tell a story about your scholarly trajectory. Many statements of purpose begin in a narrative mode, opening with a story—not about the applicant's personal life, but about her scholarship. Consider, for instance, the following hypothetical first paragraph to a statement of purpose. This paragraph illustrates how the applicant envisions her trajectory, which takes her from an undergraduate literature degree to graduate study in literature:

> *My writing had stalled. I was alone in the fifth floor of the university library in the middle of the autumn semester, my laptop open with a half-finished essay on Christina Rossetti's "On Sea-Side Grave" on the screen. I had written about the word repetition in this short poem. "Cold as the cold Decembers," the second stanza begins. I had written a bit about Rossetti's biography and her emplacement in Victorian literary culture. But I did not know what else to write. I felt like I was missing something. I turned to the stack of books on the table beside me. I had pulled every book about Rossetti from the shelf, and a few of the books were actually just collections of her poetry. In one such collection, I flipped to "On Sea-Side Grave." In the poem's final lines, Rossetti had*

written: "And all the rest forget, | But one remembers yet." Beside those lines, somebody had written in a cursive hand: "Remember yet. Jhn. Carpenter, 1906." I came up short, puzzling over the line. "Remember yet. Jhn. Carpenter, 1906." A moment ago, I had been trying to "read" Rossetti's poem. But here was a set of marks produced by another reader, a reader from the early twentieth century, recalling in the pages of Rossetti's lament a personal loss. Had this John Carpenter died in 1906? Had he died at sea? I couldn't be sure, exactly, but I knew at that moment that my study of literature would take a turn. My attempt to consider the formal qualities of a literary work—rhyme, repetition, and so on—felt incomplete without a consideration of how poetry lived in the world, how readers encountered it. I finished my essay by searching out marginalia in the other Rossetti collections housed in the university library. I found a few marks, although none as interesting as the first I discovered. But, more importantly, I found that night the path my research would take. I was interested, I decided, in the relationship between literature's formal, textual elements and the lived, embodied ways actual readers interacted with literary texts. I wanted to know more about reading by studying actual readers.

The applicant here tells a story, but it is not a story about her personal life. I don't know much about her university experience—her successes or failures. But I do know from this introduction what concerns her intellectually. She was a literature student studying the formal elements of poetry. Then, she became interested in the relationship between reader and text by encountering the mark of a past reader. This interest is not revolutionary in literary studies. The Cambridge scholar I.A. Richards studied the experiences of readers in the 1920s, and recent scholars such as Leah Price and Andrew Stauffer have made strides in this area of research. But, as an incoming graduate student, this applicant is not supposed to offer up a wholly revolutionary method of study. Rather, she is attempting to locate herself in a current scholarly field by describing how she arrived at this field through her prior areas of study. Studying poetic form, in short, provided a starting point. But, over time and through the discovery of marginalia, she became interested in the experiences of readers.

As you begin to articulate your scholarly trajectory, you will want to think about what you have studied and what you hope to study. Make a list. What are your areas of interest? How have your experiences as a scholar led you to these areas of interest? Once you have a clear sense of where you have been and where you would like to go, it will be valuable to find a crystalizing incident or set of incidents that bridge the gap between your past and your future.

It is appropriate to lightly fictionalize—but not lie—about such incidents. For instance, the student above might not really have discovered her interest in readers at the precise moment she discovered the marginalia in the poetry collection. She might have written the essay, received feedback, reflected on what she had done, and only later realized how important readers were to her intellectual trajectory. In real life, discoveries don't unfold as neatly as in stories. But the broad contours of her story should be true: She really wrote an essay about Rossetti, she really discovered the marginalia she describes, she really wrote about it in her essay, and she really does hope to study such reading practices in the future.

Ultimately, your statement about your scholarly trajectory should set up the next element of your statement of purpose: focus.

Step Two
Focus

What do you hope to study in your graduate program? The question is at once simple and maddeningly difficult to answer. Note that I am not asking the topic of your dissertation. For programs outside of the United States, students are often expected to apply with a clearly articulated dissertation project in mind. But US graduate programs instead ask students to articulate a set of methods and questions that interest them. Ideally, you should be able sum up this scholarly focus in one or two sentences, and then go on to explain why it matters to you and why it should matter to the broader scholarly community. Consider a few examples:

> *During my period of graduate study, I plan to examine how nineteenth-century racism was taught to nineteenth-century people: through geography education, popular fiction, visual culture, and even household management instruction. In short, I am interested less in how racial ideas are formulated than I am in how ordinary people come to incorporate such racist ideas into their everyday worldview.*

Or

> *Over the course of my Ph.D. program, I will examine how nineteenth-century readers read, memorized, rewrote, and remembered poetry. Rather than examining the formal qualities of such poems, I am interested in how readers themselves shaped the lives of poems across decades and generations.*

Both of these statements quickly articulate an area of interest and imply a set of methodological concerns. These are not dissertation projects, but one could very easily imagine them becoming dissertation projects after a year or two of study. Right now, the hypothetical applicants have articulated areas of focus (nineteenth-century racism, readers of poetry) that will shape their study over two years of coursework, ultimately culminating in a reading list and dissertation project.

This one- or two-sentence statement will be the most important of your entire statement of purpose, and it is worthwhile to spend a considerable amount of time writing and rewriting it. What, precisely, do you hope to study? What interests you, specifically? Getting this statement right will enable you to make clear where you're headed. It will also enable you to make the case for the importance of your scholarly interests.

And, indeed, clarifying the importance of your focus will be the key to getting your "focus" paragraph right. After making a statement about what, specifically, you hope to study, you should move on to the question of why you want to study this problem or set of problems. Your explanation should not be personal or idiosyncratic. ("I've always loved poetry," for instance, or "I've always hated racists.") Rather, your goal is to make clear the larger scholarly and social importance of this work. Consider, for instance, how the above applicant articulates the importance of her scholarly focus on poetry.

> *Over the course of my Ph.D. program, I will examine how nineteenth-century readers read, memorized, rewrote, and remembered poetry. Rather than examining the formal qualities of such poems, I am interested in how readers themselves shaped the lives of poems across decades and generations. My scholarly interest in the reception of poems, rather than in their formal qualities, in many ways marks a return to the origins of literary studies. The scholar I.A. Richards famously studied how Cambridge University students read and understood poetry in the 1920s. But as Richards became a key source for the so-called New Critics of the mid-twentieth century, his formalist approach to language took center stage. And, indeed, the study of poetry has in the intervening century been dominated by formalists, who are*

In a short series of sentences, the applicant not only makes clear what she hopes to study, but why it is important in an intellectual sense. Note here that "importance" is narrowly defined. She does not promise to end nuclear weapons proliferation or to put an end to racism or misogyny. Rather, she hopes to shed light on what she regards as an understudied dimension of poetry—one neglected by historicists and formalists alike. Importance is here defined as that which is important to an audience of literary scholars, a group she hopes to enter.

As you develop your statement of scholarly focus, you will have to make clear to your audience why you believe your area of scholarly focus is important *to those in the field you hope to enter.* You might also offer thoughts about how this area of focus is important beyond its scholarly field, in the larger world of society, politics, or world affairs. But do not lose sight of your primary audience, the scholars in your field. Your work should be situated in relation to their work. It should answer their ongoing interests and concerns.

Step three

Accomplishments

So far, you have articulated your scholarly trajectory and your scholarly focus, but how do you reassure the selection committee that you have the requisite skills, training, and character to complete a doctoral program of study? Some applicants try to convey that they are hard workers, but many students applying for graduate study have worked hard. Moreover, hard work itself is not necessarily the primary character trait required for graduate study. There will be long hours, certainly, but graduate students are often expected to be innovated thinkers, as well as thoughtful and reflective scholars. There are many paths to success in a graduate program, and many different personality traits enable success.

You should reassure the graduate admissions committee that you are prepared to succeed, then, by describing the process by which you accomplished your scholarly goals in the past. I suggest that you should discuss the process by which you achieved past goals, in part, because merely listing accomplishments will do no more than your curriculum vitae has already done. This curriculum vitae, or CV, will be submitted with your application alongside your statement of purpose, and it will list your academic degree(s), any awards you have received, any scholarly conferences you have attended, and perhaps even the courses you have taken. But no applicant for graduate school has a particularly long list of conferences and awards. It takes years for professional academics to accumulate these accomplishments. But applicants *do* have a clear memory of the process by which they went about writing essays for classes, completing research projects, and even preparing for the one or more academic conferences that they have attended.

Instead of worrying about whether you have the requisite accomplishments, then, you should focus on how you went about accomplishing past goals. What was your process like? What worked? What didn't? And what did you learn? An applicant who has presented at five conferences, but who isn't reflective about this

14

experience, is ultimately less impressive than an applicant who has never attended an academic conference but is extremely thoughtful about what they learned conducting a long-term research project for a course.

Typically, your statement about past accomplishments will be short. Again, the admissions committee has your curriculum vitae. Moreover, the statement of purpose is primarily concerned with the future: future research projects, future goals. The past, then, is relevant as a means of assessing those future goals. To that end, I urge you to stress the process by which you achieved past goals, rather than the impressiveness of your accomplishments. Consider the following hypothetical statement on process:

> *In the final year of my undergraduate English major, I completed a senior capstone thesis on the poetry of Christina Rossetti. In this thesis, I wrote about those poems I had already considered in earlier essays written for coursework, such as "On Sea-Side Grave." But, in order to take a more comprehensive view, I attempted to study how Rossetti's poetry lived on after her death in 1894. I examined library accession records in the region around my university, corresponding with research librarians and discovering that many people in my local community left collections of Rossetti's poetry to nearby libraries upon their own deaths. I examined the marginalia in these poems, often finding that readers marked stressed and unstressed syllables, noted particular passages with X-marks, and even wrote short memorials in the marginal space beside Rossetti's verse. And I examined retrospective accounts of Rossetti's life and work in British and American newspapers of the late nineteenth and early twentieth centuries. Ultimately, I argued that Rossetti's poetry provided a means through which individual readers accounted for their experiences of grief and loss. People learned to articulate their own experience of longing or suffering by channeling Rossetti's words. While I was ultimately pleased with the thesis as I wrote it, I also*

learned valuable skills through this research. I learned to track various book editions across libraries and to trace accession records. I created a system for cataloguing marginalia, allowing me to examine at scale how readers marked their reading practices. And I even learned to distinguish various kinds of ink and practices of handwriting. This project, ultimately, is a small piece of the kind of work I hope to pursue in graduate school.

Note here that the writer focuses not on the argument of her thesis—although she does note the argument. Rather, she focuses on her writing process, the skills she developed through this process, and her ultimate aims. Note also that she chooses to focus on a single accomplishment: her undergraduate thesis. While she might have won awards, written other essays, or even attended conferences, she chooses to shape her discussion of past experiences around a single text.

If this applicant submitted the undergraduate thesis as her writing sample, then discussing the skills she acquired in the process of drafting this writing sample would be a particularly apt choice. She is calling attention to what is innovative and impressive about her own work. A reviewer might miss how uncommon it is to encounter an undergraduate who has contacted numerous libraries in an attempt to discover how books of poetry circulated. By calling attention to this research in her statement of purpose, however, she is making clear to her reviewers that she has conducted this research on her own and that she has acquired various research skills in the process.

When you describe your past accomplishments to the admissions committee, your goal is not to impress them with objective criteria (i.e., "I was the first undergraduate to win this award," "I presented at four national conferences," "I wrote the longest essay in class.") If some objective measure is important to you, and not clear from your CV, you can mention it briefly before moving on. But, as a general rule, undergraduate applicants describing the impressiveness of their accomplishments simply sound boastful.

Instead, you should focus on what you have learned from your accomplishments, and how you have gone about accomplishing your goals. A thoughtfully written, methodologically innovative scholarly essay is far more impressive than any award or fellowship. Show the admissions committee not merely what you have done, but how you have done it. What was your process? What did you learn? What will you take away from these past accomplishments as a means of shaping your future accomplishments?

Step four

Aims

At this point, we have discussed your scholarly trajectory, your scholarly focus, and your past accomplishments. Now, it is time to discuss your aims. In essence, you are asked in this portion of the statement to describe the kind of scholar you hope to become. Often, this is interpreted by applicants to be a five- or ten-year career plan, with professional benchmarks clearly established. First, the Ph.D. Then, a tenure-track job. Then, tenure. But most applicants to humanities graduate programs hope to become tenure-track faculty members, a goal that is becoming increasingly difficult to realize. To distinguish yourself from other applicants, you should discuss the sort of *scholar* you hope to become, irrespective of your aim of becoming a university professor. Many scholars today work in fields adjacent to university teaching, but nonetheless continue to publish scholarly books and articles, and to give lectures to scholarly and public audiences. Neither you nor the admissions committee can predict the future. Will you teach at a Research One university or a small teaching college, or will you leave academe proper to work for a humanities nonprofit? We simply do not know. But we *can* know that you plan to join those scholars who are theorizing the rise of reactionary politics, or the history of dance, or the role of graffiti in urban culture from antiquity to the present.

Your task, then, is to articulate your scholarly aims by making clear the community of scholars you plan to join. Who is doing the sort of scholarship that you hope to extend? Why is this scholarship meaningful or important? In what direction do you hope to see it develop?

While most of the requirements of the statement of purpose demand that you look inward—to your past experiences, your future goals, your scholarly interests—the "aims" section will require you to look outward. What scholarly communities are focused on the questions that draw your interest? Who are the scholars focused on these questions? You might have a clear sense of the answers to these questions based on a past research project. If you are like most applicants, however, you'll have only the vaguest idea of what the scholarly field looks like as a present-tense, working reality. A good place to start, then, is with the programs you hope to enter.

Let's say you're interested in cognitive literary theory, also known as cognitive poetics. This scholarly movement emerged in the 1990s and in the first decade of the twenty-first century. Scholars in this subfield deploy evolutionary biology and cognitive science to understand how patterns in language and storytelling recur across cultures, languages, and historical periods. Many undergraduates become familiar with cognitive poetics, if they become familiar with it at all, through the names of a few famous scholars, such as Reuven Tsur and Ronald Langacker. But, as an applicant, you'll want to be familiar with the full field, particularly those who are currently publishing in it. You'll also want to know which of these current scholars are likely to accept graduate students. Do they actively teach in a graduate program? Do they supervise dissertations? (This information should be on their department's website, and you'll find more discussion of this question in the next section: Fit.) As you research the field of cognitive literary theory, you'll come across the names of numerous active scholars, including Lisa Zunshine, Patrick Colm Hogan, and Mark Turner. You'll want to read some of their work to develop a familiarity with it. Then, as you write your statement, you'll want to indicate how your scholarly interests align with the questions that they are asking in their own work. In essence, you're communicating that you are an apprentice scholar within a recognizable community of scholars. Your questions and concerns, ultimately, align with theirs.

Consider, alternatively, the hypothetical applicant who has developed an interest in nineteenth-century readers and readership. She began by discussing marginalia in nineteenth-century books, such as collections of poems by Christina Rossetti. She will want to consider the contemporary scholars publishing on questions of readership and marginalia right now. Such scholars include Leah Price, Rita Felski, and Andrew Stauffer. Our hypothetical applicant might write:

> *I am not alone in my believing that a better understanding of how readers actually read will reshape how scholars understand literary texts. In recent years, Rita Felski has called for scholars to reconsider "critique," the dominant mode in literary studies, and to think of literary texts as productive. Felski has suggested that, rather than searching out how texts function as vectors for ideology and mystification, scholars should think about how literary texts build relationships, communities, and new possibilities for seeing the world. Similarly, Leah Price has called for a renewed attention to actual readers. Price's observation that even blank pages might indicate readerly absorption—in that focused readers don't write notes in the margins—has been a particular challenge to my interest in marginalia. Finally, Andrew Stauffer's recent studies of marginalia in American texts, particularly late-nineteenth-century texts, has shaped my own approach to understanding how readers have understood poetry. Collectively, these scholars have challenged both formalist and narrowly historicist approaches to the literary archive, calling upon us to study how readers imbue texts with hope, possibility, and futurity. These scholars are concerned, as I am concerned, with the ways literary texts enable readers to produce and record new knowledge, new meaning, and new possibilities.*

Note here that the applicant has not entirely turned away from her own interests and views. She has not allowed the other scholars to take over the statement, but she has made clear the relationship between her approach and their approaches. Moreover, she has demonstrated a real engagement with the writing of these scholars. She has likely spent some time thinking about the work of Felski,

Price, and Stauffer. She has not conflated their work. Rather, she has given a short sentence to each, noting at the end of the paragraph how these scholars collectively form a community to which she should belong.

Would the scholars recognize themselves as part of a single community? Perhaps, or perhaps not. Working scholars are often communicating with colleagues in many different subfields. Stauffer communicates with scholars who study the history of reading, scholars of nineteenth-century sentimentality, scholars of English Romanticism and American literary and cultural studies, scholars of the digital humanities, and so on. Likewise, Felski and Price are located in various, different subfields.

The applicant demonstrates her ability to construct a scholarly community by finding the intersections between the work of those scholars who interest her. She wants to build upon the work of Felski, Price, and Stauffer, and so she finds a way of linking the three through their interest in readers. Piecing together this community of scholars, moreover, will also enable her to identify the universities to which she will apply. Since Stauffer and Felski are both currently professors at the University of Virginia, the applicant might seriously consider that university as a potential intellectual home as she pursues her Ph.D. I do not mean to imply, however, that you can only name those professors to whose programs you will apply. You should place yourself within a field, not merely within a department, and you should note the work of major scholars across various universities.

Ultimately, your task is to show that you belong in a current, interesting, and wide-ranging scholarly community. You demonstrate this by naming those scholars who you imagine as your future interlocutors, showing how they are linked, and showing how the questions you ask in your scholarship align with the questions they ask in their scholarship.

Step Five
Fit

You have articulated your scholarly trajectory: How you will move from the scholar you were to the scholar you plan to become. You have articulated your scholarly focus: What sorts of questions interest you and engage you, and why are they important? You have made clear how your past accomplishments augur future success, not because they are impressive but because you learned important lessons in the process of producing this earlier scholarship. And you have made clear your aim to join a current, vital, and active field of scholars working on a particular set of important questions.

But why should *this particular* university admit you to their program. Well, because you're a great fit. You don't just fit with the aims and goals of any humanist program, but with the aims and goals of *this particular* program. Your "fit" paragraph should be tailored to each application you submit, and it should answer how your proposed trajectory aligns with the aims of the institution and with the scholarly interests of particular faculty members.

Rather than attempting to write this paragraph immediately, you should research the institution. Does the department value particular questions over others? For instance, some English Ph.D. programs aren't strictly literature programs. Instead, they offer a Ph.D. in "English and Cultural Studies," or a Ph.D. in "Rhetoric, Writing, and Culture." These communicate very different values. The former program is interested in literary studies as a form of cultural studies, probably in the tradition of Raymond Williams and the Birmingham School. This program will be interested in examining culture broadly, through literature and other forms of cultural production. You might expect professors to teach courses on Dime Novels, comic books, cinema, and other kinds of "lowbrow" literatures, as a means of understanding the operations of race, capitalism, or other forms of power. By contrast, the latter program ("Rhetoric, Writing, and Culture") isn't really a literature program at all. It is interested in training Ph.D. students to direct programs in Rhetoric and Writing, but it likely also has a cultural studies component that enables graduates to occasionally teach literature classes. A program that uses none of these keywords—"cultural studies," "rhetoric," or "writing"—is going to be more strictly literary in its focus. A Ph.D. in "literature" or "literature and letters" will likely be more focused on what is commonly understood as literature—that is, high culture.

History and philosophy programs often similarly communicate their aims and goals, but they tend to be a bit less coded in how they communicate this information. Is the history program linked to an American Studies or ethnic studies program, for instance? If so, the department will likely have a tremendous focus on the history of race. Or, conversely, is the program linked to a center for European history, or a center for Chinese history? These centers and programs will communicate the focus of the department. Where do they put their resources?

You will also want to know if the university is linked to particular archives or libraries. The University of Texas at Austin, for instance, hosts the Harry Ransom Center, one of the premier archives for American history and culture in the United States. You could certainly attend UT to study European literature or the history of medieval Greece. But the American history and American literature students there benefit tremendously from having access to a major archive. A student there might even hope to make a wholly new archival discovery during their doctoral work—the sort of discovery that makes it into the pages of major newspapers and magazines.

As much as the institution is important, though, the faculty are more important. You will want to demonstrate that your research aims align with three or more faculty in the department. First, though, you'll need to decide who is active in the department. Often, you'll see a list of thirty, forty, or even more faculty members, but not all of these faculty members actually work with graduate students.

To find out which faculty are eligible to work with graduate students, you'll need to know their rank.

In the American academy, there are two separate groups of faculty members at a research university. The first group are temporary, contingent, or teaching-focused faculty members, and they *do not* work with graduate students. If a professor's title is:

- adjunct professor
- visiting assistant professor
- teaching professor
- professor of practice
- lecturer
- instructor

then they almost certainly do not teach or advise graduate students. You should not mention them in your statement of purpose. The second group includes permanent faculty members who *do* advise graduate students. A scholar entering this group is:

- first appointed as assistant professor
- advances to associate professor when they receive tenure
- then advances to professor (typically after the publication of their second book with an academic press)
- and may then advance to a named professorship (i.e., the Phillis Jones Professor of European History)
- or may even advance to a "sterling" or "university" professorship, the highest possible rank (i.e., "the Phillis Jones University Professor of European History)

Anybody from this second group, from assistant professor to university professor, is theoretically available to advise graduate students. But do they? You'll want to check the list of recent Ph.D. graduates to see if this faculty member continues to advise students. You'll also want to check the list of recent courses to see if this person teaches graduate seminars. From there, you will make a list of those professors in the department who are: A.) eligible to advise graduate students, and B.) actively teaching or advising graduate students. In your statement of purpose, *you only want to mention by name those professors who actively work with graduate students.*

There are many reasons that a professor eligible to work with graduate students might not work with them. In one department I know of, a popular and highly published professor had a child with severe disabilities. After his child was born, the department agreed to allow him to step back from graduate advising, which is extremely time intensive, for several years so that he could focus on his family. For applicants to the program, this meant that the well-known professor simply wasn't available to advise projects, although he eventually returned to graduate advising. In another department I know of, a professor had so many personality conflicts with graduate students that the director of graduate studies asked him to step away from graduate teaching altogether. You simply do not know why a faculty member who *could* advise graduate students isn't actually advising them. You don't want to imperil your chances of admission by listing a faculty member who isn't actually going to take new advisees.

I would like to offer a word of caution about assistant professors, as well. Often, these professors have the most current, exciting, and innovative work in the department. But they are also imperfect choices as major advisors for graduate students. Elite universities do not award tenure to all of their junior faculty. An assistant professor has a six-year probationary window from the time they are hired to the time they go up for promotion. If they do not get promoted, with tenure, they are often asked to leave the university. Brilliant, capable scholars often do not receive tenure. Indeed, in many cases, tenure is denied because a book's publication schedule ran behind. If an assistant professor's tenure review is scheduled for May 2022, but her scholarly monograph isn't available for sale until July 2022, she might not be given tenure and, as a result, she might lose her job. If you are an applicant to be her advisee, faculty in the department might already be wondering if she will stay on at the university. They might be reluctant to admit students to work with a junior colleague they believe is unlikely to receive tenure. As an applicant, you have no way of knowing these internal politics. Consequently, you should mention no more than one assistant professor in your statement of purpose.

So far, you have looked at the list of assistant professors, associate professors, professors, chaired professors, and university professors. By looking at the current list of graduate advisors and the professors in recent graduate courses, you have determined which of these professors actually work with graduate students. From this list, you should choose three, or perhaps four, faculty members with whom your work aligns. You will mention these scholars in the "fit" paragraph of your statement of purpose.

But what will this fit paragraph actually look like? Ideally, your fit paragraph will have four parts:

> 1.) You will explain why your scholarly goals align with those of the department.
> 2.) You will explain why your scholarly goals align with a particular archive, center, or research focus within the department.
> 3.) You will suggest how your scholarship aligns with three or four faculty members in the department.
> 4.) You will close by articulating your enthusiasm for joining the department.

These four parts will not be even. Parts one, two, and four will likely only take up one or two sentences each. But part three—the part where you align your scholarship with the work of other scholars in the department—will require that you articulate why each scholar's work is interesting and why it aligns with your research focus.

Consider the hypothetical applicant we have been following across the pages of this guide. She was writing about marginalia in nineteenth-century poetry, describing how she hoped to work on the history of readers and reading. She will attempt to link her scholarly interests to those of the faculty in the English

Department, but also to the values and interests of the department itself. She might write a "fit" statement such as this:

> *And this is why the English Department at the University of X is an excellent fit for my future scholarship. Through its Center for Literary History, founded three years ago, the department has recommitted itself to the study of literature as a shaping influence on historical events, and as a graduate student I would aim to contribute to the research programs and colloquia organized by that center. Moreover, my scholarly aims align with a number of faculty in the department. Professor X.O. Smith's recent work on late-eighteenth-century circulating libraries has brought renewed attention to reading as a social practice, one shaped by commercial institutions and codes of conduct. This perspective would enrich my research on Victorian-era reading practices by providing a prehistory to the reading practices I have encountered in my scholarship. Professor J.R. Nguyen, moreover, has called attention through her scholarship to the trans-historical influence of literary forms: how the sonnet or the bildungsroman is not only a product of its time, but a shaping influence upon the cultural forms of later times. My interest in how readers return again and again to old literary forms would benefit from collaboration and study with Professor Nguyen. Finally, I would be eager to work with Professor P.R. Francois, whose research on the emergence of the New Criticism, and formalism more generally, would provide important context for my work urging a turn away from narrowly formalist or narrowly historicist scholarship. Only by understanding formalism as an attempt to solve a particular set of intellectual and aesthetic problems, I suggest, might we understand how to approach literary form differently—from the perspective of readers. Ultimately, the English Department at the University of X has demonstrated a commitment to understanding literary texts as historical*

Note here that the applicant spends a significant amount of space describing the work of each professor and linking her own scholarship to their work. She moves from a statement of fit, to a discussion of the department's new Center for Literary History, to a discussion of each faculty member, to a statement of her eagerness to join the department.

Note also that she does not identify an advisor, as she would have to if she were applying to a university in the United Kingdom or Europe. Instead, she lists three professors who might be potential advisors. Perhaps Professor Smith is no longer taking advisees, but Professor Nguyen and Professor Francois have several openings. The applicant doesn't know this, but by mentioning all three she enables the committee to place her most advantageously. Once the applicant enrolls in the university, she can decide who she'd like to work with. But listing three potential mentors enables the admissions committee to imagine that the student will have a stable place in their program. A personality conflict, an illness, or a retirement won't irrevocably harm the applicant's studies. She will have several potential mentors.

The "fit" paragraph is an opportunity to praise the department by highlighting what you admire about it and its faculty, but it is important that this praise not be empty encomium. Often, early drafts of "fit" statements include gratuitous adjectives: the faculty are "brilliant," "extraordinary," or "stunning." The problem with this sort of praise is that it sounds hollow. Departments are often very clear about what they think they do well, and about what they're not interested in doing. The department with the Center for the Study of Medieval Manuscripts is likely quite proud of the rigorous historicism of its scholarship, and of the resources commanded by such a center. Simply calling the department "brilliant" will make it seem like you don't understand what actually makes the program extraordinary. Make specific, verifiable statements about the department and its faculty. You've chosen this university for a reason. Why?

Ultimately, the fit paragraph answers a very specific question. Out of hundreds of applicants, they will winnow the field down to a small group that they regard as highly qualified potential graduate students. They cannot admit all of these qualified applicants, however. The difference between an admission and a rejection usually comes down to fit. Will this applicant thrive with the opportunity provided by this particular program? Will her scholarly interests align with those of our faculty? Will she benefit from the institutional structures available here: archives, centers, and certificate programs? Your task is to make clear to the admissions committee that you would indeed fit well in their program.

Final Thoughts

Applicants who follow the process outlined in this guide often find that it doesn't have space for things they'd like to explain to the committee. Perhaps they have a weakness in their application that needs explaining, or perhaps they have an extremely limited word count for the statement of purpose. Statements might be limited to 1,500 words, to 1,000 words, or even to 500 words. Below, then, I'll offer a few thoughts about how this model might be adapted to include explanations of a weaker applicant profile or a shorter word count.

Weaknesses in your application

Often, applicants hope to use their statement of purpose as a means of explaining the weaker elements of their academic record: bad grades, weak letters of recommendation, a long delay between degrees. This approach is perfectly acceptable, but I would offer a few cautions.

First, not every element of your application that you perceive as weak is actually weak. I once had a literature professor who confessed that she simply skipped the quantitative portion of the Graduate Record Examination—receiving a zero on that portion of the test. Why? She preferred to be thought of as a rebel than as stupid. I don't recommend this particular strategy, but the larger point remains. Even with a zero, elite graduate programs accepted her. Her ability in mathematics was simply not relevant. She went on to have an extraordinary career as a scholar and poet, and her GRE score has become part of a joke she tells at parties. Likewise, a grade in your chemistry course or in computer programming will likely have little bearing on your success in graduate study in the humanities.

That said, perhaps you have struggled *in the humanities*. In that case, you might find it worthwhile to explain this struggle. But your goal here isn't to make excuses. Remember from step three, accomplishments, that the admissions committee is more interested in the steps you have taken to accomplish your goals than in

measuring your accomplishments objectively. When members of
the admissions committee faculty have won the Bancroft Prize or
the Pulitzer, have given invited lectures in Paris and Vienna and
Honolulu, and have written books and appeared in documentary
films, you're unlikely to impress them merely with your
undergraduate record. Your task is to show them how you think
about the process of going about accomplishing your aims. If you
struggled in your modern poetry class, by all means explain why.
But explain yourself with an eye to the future. What did you learn
from this experience, and how will this change your future course
of study?

The goal here is not to demonstrate that you are an
impressive person. You haven't yet accomplished the great things
that you are going to accomplish. That's why you're applying to
graduate school. Rather, the goal is to demonstrate that you are
thoughtful about your successes and your failures, and that you
regard both as part of a process by which you will achieve your
scholarly and intellectual aims.

Word counts

One of the most frustrating things about applying to
graduate school is that the statement of purpose word counts and
instructions vary widely. My recommendation is that you begin by
writing a long-ish (1,000- to 1,400-word) statement over the course
of the summer before application season. You will write the "fit"
paragraph with placeholder language, to be filled in with specifics
later. Then, you will have a skeleton of the statement that you will
provide to each university. As you select the ten or more
institutions to which you plan to apply, you will tailor each
statement to the instructions from that institution.

Many institutions will require a slightly shorter statement:
say, 1,000 words. To accomplish this, you will cut a word here and
a sentence there, reducing the overall word count to precisely
1,000.

The real problem comes up when an institution requires an extremely short statement: say, 500 words. In this case, your five-part statement simply won't work. First, cut the statement about your scholarly trajectory. The institution *must* know your focus. This is the most important part of your application, and so you should begin here. You might also cut aggressively from your past accomplishments, as these are covered in the curriculum vitae. The remainder—focus, aims, fit—can be trimmed down to the 500-word maximum. Such a short statement is, I think, unfortunate, but such institutions are communicating that they want to know in very specific terms what you plan to accomplish while at their institution.

***

Ultimately, the statement of purpose is an opportunity to explain yourself as an intellectual, as a thinker who will go on to develop an innovative research program. You are not "selling yourself," as so many guides to university applications will tell you. You are, instead, articulating a plan for future research as it relates to your past research. What have you done in the past, and how does this set up a trajectory for your future study? You should write to the admissions committee as a future colleague, as a person capable of joining them in their scholarly endeavor.

An Example Statement of Purpose

My writing had stalled. I was alone in the fifth floor of the university library in the middle of the autumn semester, my laptop open with a half-finished essay on Christina Rossetti's "On Sea-Side Grave" on the screen. I had written about the word repetition in this short poem. "Cold as the cold Decembers," the second stanza begins. I had written a bit about Rossetti's biography and her emplacement in Victorian literary culture. But I did not know what else to write. I felt like I was missing something. I turned to the stack of books on the table beside me. I had pulled every book about Rossetti from the shelf, and a few of the books were actually just collections of her poetry. In one such collection, I flipped to "On Sea-Side Grave." In the poem's final lines, Rossetti had written: "And all the rest forget, | But one remembers yet." Beside those lines, somebody had written in a cursive hand: "Remember yet. Jhn. Carpenter, 1906." I came up short, puzzling over the line. "Remember yet. Jhn. Carpenter, 1906." A moment ago, I had been trying to "read" Rossetti's poem. But here was a set of marks produced by another reader, a reader from the early twentieth century, recalling in the pages of Rossetti's lament a personal loss. Had this John Carpenter died in 1906? Had he died at sea? I couldn't be sure, exactly, but I knew at that moment that my study of literature would take a turn. My attempt to consider the formal qualities of a literary work—rhyme, repetition, and so on—felt incomplete without a consideration of how poetry lived in the world, how readers encountered it. I finished my essay by searching out marginalia in the other Rossetti collections housed in the university library. I found a few marks, although none as interesting as the first I discovered. But, more importantly, I found that night the path my research would take. I was interested, I decided, in the relationship between literature's formal, textual elements and the lived, embodied ways actual readers interacted with literary texts. I wanted to know more about reading by studying actual readers.

Over the course of my Ph.D. program, I will examine how nineteenth-century readers read, memorized, rewrote, and remembered poetry. Rather than examining the formal qualities of such poems, I am interested in how readers themselves shaped the lives of poems across decades and generations. My scholarly interest in the reception of poems, rather than in their formal qualities, in many ways marks a return to the origins of literary studies. The scholar I.A. Richards famously studied how Cambridge University students read and understood poetry in the 1920s. But as Richards became a key source for the so-called New Critics of the mid-twentieth century, his formalist approach to language took center stage. And, indeed, the study of poetry has in the intervening century been dominated by formalists, who are interested in the poem as an autonomous object, and historicists, who locate the poem in the time of its original composition or publication. Yet poems exert influence across time, and they shape and are shaped by the minds and hearts of individual readers. Recent scholars, such as Leah Price and Andrew Stauffer, have called attention to the trans-historical dimensions of poetry, and I hope to extend and continue their work by returning us to a consideration of the poem's primary audience, the reader.

In the final year of my undergraduate English major, I completed a senior capstone thesis on the poetry of Christina Rossetti. In this thesis, I wrote about those poems I had already considered in earlier essays written for coursework, such as "On Sea-Side Grave." But, in order to take a more comprehensive view, I attempted to study how Rossetti's poetry lived on after her death in 1894. I examined library accession records in the region around my university, corresponding with research librarians and discovering that many people in my local community left collections of Rossetti's poetry to nearby libraries upon their own deaths. I examined the marginalia in these poems, often finding that readers marked stressed and unstressed syllables, noted particular passages with X-marks, and even wrote short memorials in the marginal space beside Rossetti's verse. And I examined retrospective accounts of Rossetti's life and work in British and American newspapers of the late nineteenth and early twentieth centuries. Ultimately, I argued that Rossetti's poetry provided a means through which individual readers accounted for their experiences of grief and loss. People learned to articulate their own experience of longing or suffering by channeling Rossetti's words. While I was ultimately pleased with the thesis as I wrote it, I also learned valuable skills through this research. I learned to track various book editions across libraries and to trace accession records. I created a system for cataloguing marginalia, allowing me to examine at scale how readers marked their reading practices. And I even learned to distinguish various kinds of ink and practices of handwriting. This project, ultimately, is a small piece of the kind of work I hope to pursue in graduate school.

I am not alone in my believing that a better understanding of how readers actually read will reshape how scholars understand literary texts. In recent years, Rita Felski has called for scholars to reconsider "critique," the dominant mode in literary studies, and to think of literary texts as productive. Felski has suggested that, rather than searching out how texts function as vectors for ideology and mystification, scholars should think about how literary texts build relationships, communities, and new possibilities for seeing the world. Similarly, Leah Price has called for a renewed attention to actual readers. Price's observation that even blank pages might indicate readerly absorption—in that focused readers don't write notes in the margins—has been a particular challenge to my interest in marginalia. Finally, Andrew Stauffer's recent studies of marginalia in American texts, particularly late-nineteenth-century texts, has shaped my own approach to understanding how readers have understood poetry. Collectively, these scholars have challenged both formalist and narrowly historicist approaches to the literary archive, calling upon us to study how readers imbue texts with hope, possibility, and futurity. These scholars are concerned, as I am concerned, with the ways literary texts enable readers to produce and record new knowledge, new meaning, and new possibilities.

And this is why the English Department at the University of X is an excellent fit for my future scholarship. Through its Center for Literary History, founded three years ago, the department has recommitted itself to the study of literature as a shaping influence on historical events, and as a graduate student I would aim to contribute to the research programs and colloquia organized by that center. Moreover, my scholarly aims align with a number of faculty in the department. Professor X.O. Smith's recent work on late-eighteenth-century circulating libraries has brought renewed attention to reading as a social practice, one shaped by commercial institutions and codes of conduct. This perspective would enrich my research on Victorian-era reading practices by providing a prehistory to the reading practices I have encountered in my scholarship. Professor J.R. Nguyen, moreover, has called attention through her scholarship to the trans-historical influence of literary forms: how the sonnet or the bildungsroman is not only a product of its time, but a shaping influence upon the cultural forms of later times. My interest in how readers return again and again to old literary forms would benefit from collaboration and study with Professor Nguyen. Finally, I would be eager to work with Professor P.R. Francois, whose research on the emergence of the New Criticism, and formalism more generally, would provide important context for my work urging a turn away from narrowly formalist or narrowly historicist scholarship. Only by understanding formalism as an attempt to solve a particular set of intellectual and aesthetic problems, I suggest, might we understand how to approach literary form differently—from the perspective of readers. Ultimately, the English Department at the University of X has demonstrated a commitment to understanding literary texts as historical agents, forms that exert a shaping influence on culture and on people over time. I believe this mode of inquiry to be extremely important, and I am eager to join this intellectually rich scholarly community.

Notes for your statement of purpose

www.ingramcontent.com/pod-product-compliance
Lightning Source LLC
Chambersburg PA
CBHW051134250726
48655CB00007B/3058